To:-

From:-

D0893485

OTHER BOOKS IN THE TO-GIVE-AND-TO-KEEP® SERIES:

To a Very Special Dad
To a Very Special Friend
To my Very Special Love
To a Very Special Granddaughter
Happy Anniversary
To a Very Special Son
Wishing You Happiness
To a Very Special Daughter
To my Very Special Husband

Merry Christmas
To a Very Special Grandma
To a Very Special Sister
To my Very Special Wife
To a Very Special Grandpa
To a Very Special Grandson
To a Very Special Brother
To a Special Couple on your
  Wedding Day

EDITED BY HELEN EXLEY.

Published simultaneously in 1994 by Exley Publications in Great Britain,
and Exley Giftbooks in the USA.

12 11 10 9 8 7 6 5 4 3 2

© Helen Exley 1994.
The moral right of the author has been asserted.

ISBN 1-86187-367-0

Exley Publications Ltd, 16 Chalk Hill, Watford, Herts WD19 4BG, UK.
Exley Publications LLC, 232 Madison Avenue, Suite 1409, NY 10016, USA.
www.helenexleygiftbooks.com

'TO A VERY SPECIAL'® AND 'TO-GIVE-AND-TO-KEEP'®
ARE REGISTERED TRADE MARKS OF EXLEY PUBLICATIONS LTD
AND EXLEY PUBLICATIONS LLC.

Welcome to the NEW BABY

WRITTEN BY PAM BROWN
ILLUSTRATED BY JULIETTE CLARKE

Look at this wonder! Perfect. Beautiful.

Mouth, ears, rounded little feet.

Hands clenched against the world.

Yours.

A new life fashioned from your love.

. . .

A HELEN EXLEY GIFTBOOK

EXLEY
NEW YORK • WATFORD, UK

<u>WELCOME, LITTLE ONE</u>

The birth of a new baby is like unwrapping a
package that has intrigued you for the best part of a
year – and finding its contents more exciting, more
perfect, more wonderful than you ever dreamed.

. . .

You planned the baby. You read all the books.
You went to all the classes.
A nursery waiting, fresh papered, painted. Talcs and
oils and teddy bears. Warmth and welcome.
And yet – to hold the reality safe in your arms and
heart is always an astonishment.
Where there was supposed to be a baby there
is a special person.

. . .

All the new baby needs at first is food,

warmth and sleep.

It is so small, so perfect, so new –

so utterly helpless.

You do your best - nervous, a little bewildered

by its self-absorbed demands, and

conscious of your gigantic size and

utter inexperience.

And then, one day, the eyes find your face, focus

and light up with recognition.

And a smile like no other, a smile of pure joy and

utter trust sweeps away all confusion,

all awkwardness.

And you begin the long, glad journey of discovery.

. . .

NOTHING WILL EVER BE THE SAME

Of course you will be deeply involved in your work,

in your friendships, your interests, the world about

you. Just as you always have been.

Except that from now there will always be a priority.

A corner of the mind occupied with another issue.

The core of life has shifted.

It lies in your arms.

. . .

A baby extends the concept of Us.

. . .

Living together gave you shared silences, quiet talk,
easy companionship, leisurely Sunday lunches.
Now you must learn to love in a different way – in
the blurred world of night feeds, colic, sniffles,
teething, tantrums, flung food and sudden scares.
It's not so hard.
Arms reaching out to take the fretful child.
Shared fears. Shared laughter.
Silly whispered conversation in the dark, the baby
sprawled between you.
Bath times and play times. Sudden smiles.
New marvels every day – first word, first step,
first everything.
A life less simple – but richer than you could have
ever dreamed.

. . .

Once you were lovers, friends, companions.
Now you are woven at last into a family.
Inseparable.

. . .

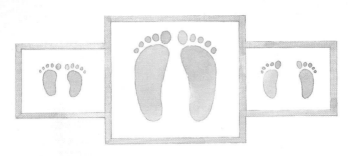

ONE SMILE IS ENOUGH

You have made a hundred resolutions about
"starting as we mean to go on" and "kindly but
firm" and "one must not allow the child to dominate
one's whole existence."

It smiles. And there's an end to all the resolutions.

. . .

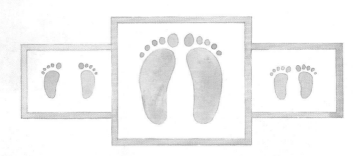

A baby has no weapons, no language, little strength.
It has only one way to defend itself – its smile. But
that has been enough to keep the human race going.

. . .

A baby's smile says "You, I remember." "You I
trust." "You I love."…. and "Please – love me too."

. . .

A baby looks at you. Blank. Bewildered. And then,
suddenly, the eyes brighten and it smiles.
A gift from the heart – and more beautiful than
any other.

. . .

Washing, ironing, cleaning, cooking – sleep lost and
days disjointed.
Babies cost a lot in nervous wear and tear.
But give one smile, and all the debt is paid.

. . .

HAPPY, HAPPY DAYS

First the child discovers light and then a face. And
for a while that face is all the world. But then
another face, and more and more, all smiling
and welcoming.

And shiny beautiful things. And flowers and trees
and dogs and cats and birds suspended in the air.

And buses, cars, men digging in the road.

And sand and sea.

But always, when night comes, those first-loved
faces – sealing the day with kisses.

The baby is the perfect excuse for doing all those things adulthood demanded you to renounce.

Now you can lie on your back and kick your legs.

Now you can make mud pies. Now you can make faces.

Now you can dance. And sing.

The sky's the limit.

And all you ask as a reward is a bubbling of laughter, a squeal of delight, or eyes suddenly wide in amazement.

. . .

A baby brings endless gifts – a new delight, a new astonishment, each day.

So small – the fulcrum of our lives,
the pivot of our universe.

. . .

Here in this cradle is your very existence.
For this small life you would gladly
give your own.
No one told you it would be like this.
No one ever can.

. . .

All the anticipation and planning in the
world does not prepare one for the reality –
this small and perfect person in your arms.
The awe of responsibility. The
overwhelming love.

. . .

One looks at one's child aged six months –
and wonders how life was ever possible
without it.

· · ·

How gently, how delicately, how lovingly a
father takes up his newborn child. An
amazed love...for he had never quite
believed in miracles.

· · ·

There is no swirl of suns more beautiful.
There is no marvel greater than a child.

· · ·

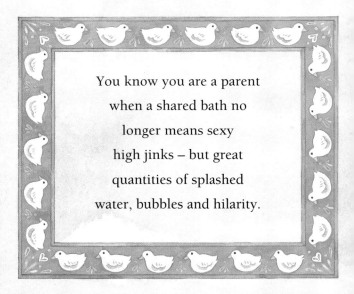

You know you are a parent
when a shared bath no
longer means sexy
high jinks – but great
quantities of splashed
water, bubbles and hilarity.

YOU KNOW YOU ARE A PARENT WHEN ...

... when going out for the day assumes the
complication of a crossing of the Sahara.

... when you discover the entire world is a death trap
for the unwary child.

... when any tragedy to do with children, anywhere
in the world, pierces you to the heart.

... when you greet a splurge of vomit down the front
of your dress with:
"*There. That's* shifted the nasty wind, *hasn't* it?"

... when it takes ten minutes to get out of the car.

... when you stop looking at displays of clothes and
shoes and makeup, and perfume – and are bewitched
by miniscule coats and gigantic teddy bears.

... when you learn that a small child takes up nine-
tenths of the space in any shared bed.

... when you discover an astounding talent for
making animal noises.

... when the washing machine never stops.

... when a tiny, *tiny* toothbrush is ranged
beside your own.

Sleep sound.
Sleep tight.
Sleep soundly
right through the night!
Please!

. . .

ALL THROUGH THE NIGHT

Your baby loves you. It likes your conversation. It
likes your company. Especially in the boring
stretches of the night.

. . .

Baby simply missed breaths.
The parents greet the dawn haggard and exhausted
– not because the baby cried – but because they
dared not go to sleep.

. . .

NIGHT FEED

The small noises begin. The snufflings, the mumblings, the lip-smackings. Perhaps it is a dream. Perhaps the sounds will all drift away to silence. Perhaps... A thin insistent wail. Ah well.

A parent stumbles out of bed.

Fed, changed.

The little head slips sideways, the eyelids flutter and close, there is a hint of blissful snoring.

Lift it gently now. Gently. Gently.

Softly asleep it lies, back in its crib.

And the blue eyes open.

And there is a smile.

How *very* good it is to see you, it says. Time for a cuddle. Time for a talk. Time for a song.

Three o'clock in the morning?

What's time to friends?

. . .

THE WORLD'S BEST AUDIENCE

Babies are popular because they are so
wonderfully easy to please. Nothing else you
do in life is greeted with such rapture as
"Ride a Cock Horse" and "Boo!"

. . .

If you have a singing voice you dare not
even raise in church, never mind. You can
sing all you like to your baby – to the best
audience in the world.

. . .

There is no more endearing sight than
a very large daddy trying to lure a smile out of a
very small baby.

. . .

Playing "Boo" around the newspaper can become
hugely monotonous. But Grandma goes on. Just to
see Baby's face dazzle with delight.

. . .

MINI DESPOTS

No human being can own another, and most particularly its own child. Of course, a baby does not yet know this fact.

It is blissfully confident that it owns you from head to boots.

. . .

Nature has tuned babies to scream at the exact pitch that turns the brain to jelly. They do not accept *any* prevarication.

Now is the message. *Now*.

. . .

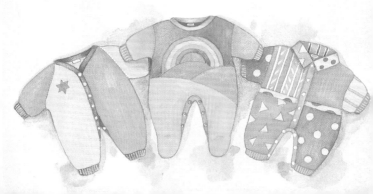

A baby whose cry has been ignored has an extra
weapon – the quivering lower lip.

. . .

A baby says
"I love you
but I must insist you rearrange your lives.
Sleep when I sleep. Eat when I am full.
Play when I am in the mood.
Cancel all previous engagements – *I* am here.
I am laying the foundation of my life and must
not be deterred.
Later, you may rest.
Later, you may take time off.
But now
feed me."

. . .

Catherine the Great was never as imperious
as a baby.

. . .

IN NEED OF CARE

No words are ever quite as
effective as a baby's cry.

. . .

The world demands much,
and gives little.
A baby asks food, warmth –
and your love.
And gives you absolute trust
and absolute love in return.

. . .

A baby is not utterly helpless. It
has a voice. It has a smile. But
these are its only protection.

. . .

May all babies' dreams be
without fear.

. . .

Every baby in the world deserves to be loved.

. . .

The sad thing is, one can't explain to animals or
babies about illness or its treatment.
They just expect you to take the misery away.

. . .

This small and perfect creature.
You want to keep it from all harm, all danger.
You want to teach it all that it has taken you a
lifetime of mistakes to learn.
But, alas, every human creature must learn these
things for itself.

. . .

The crying baby warns us – you must love me when
I cry, when I break your nights, when I take up your
time, when I answer back, when I do wrong, when I
turn from you, when I leave you.
I am yours forever.
And you are mine.

. . .

A SECOND CHANCE

Every baby is the possibility
of a better world.
It's all that keeps us going.

. . .

A baby gives us back the
world we had lost – a world
of wonders. The brightness
of a flower. The flicker of a
flame. A butterfly. A leaf. A
bird. New created.
Wonderful.
We see them through the
eyes of innocence. And the
joy of the child is ours.

. . .

To watch a baby discovering the world is to rediscover it yourself. How could you have forgotten how shiny and smooth a ball was, how water flashes light, how the leaves shift and dapple on a summer's day, how ducks upend themselves, how squirrels run across the grass?

A child makes all things new again.

. . .

How slowly the days pass by when one is very small – packed tight with wonders. Dear Mother, Father. Take a slower pace from me. See through my eyes. Rediscover all that you've forgotten – the little miracles of flower and puddle, shell and feather, pebble, rainbow, leaf.

They are my gift to you.

. . .

Only a baby can show us the strength and love and courage we have hidden in ourselves.

. . .

A SHORT, VERY PRECIOUS, TIME

For a little while the household must revolve around
the baby. Soon enough it will have to learn
discipline. For this brief magic hour – let it be the
focal point of your lives.

. . .

Dear Baby, Just for a little while your place is in my
arms, snuggled against my shoulder, sprawled
across my knees – or drifting into sleep at any angle
that you choose, your starfish hands outflung.
But even now I feel your little feet brace against
me, feel you twist like a little fish – getting ready
for escape.
The time is getting nearer when you will squirm
away across the floor, then crawl, then walk.
Then run to the furthest corners of the world.
But I will always remember.
And will always be waiting.
Just in case you need me.

. . .

Never rush a baby. It's only going this way once – let it enjoy the view.

. . .

Dear Parents, Do not begrudge me these few months of needing your absolute attention. I am busier than I will ever be again – growing and learning for my future.

And I will show my gratitude.

Every day I'll bring you something new, something wonderful. A smile, a bird sound, an achievement. My being small lasts so short a time. Share it with me. Before you know it, I'll be grown and gone.

. . .

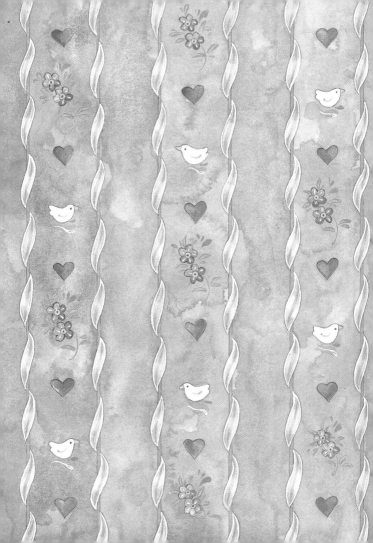